# THE
# DORSETSHIRE
# REGIMENT

The Keep, gateway to the Depot Barracks, 1905.

# THE DORSETSHIRE REGIMENT

Terry Bishop

TEMPUS

Men of 'G' Company, 1st Dorsets, returning to camp over Wool Bridge in 1909. That summer the Battalion was on manoeuvres in Wool and on Salisbury Plain, a most welcome alternative to Aldershot.

First published 1999
This edition 2006

Tempus Publishing Limited
The Mill, Brimscombe Port,
Stroud, Gloucestershire, GL5 2QG
www.tempus-publishing.com

British Library Cataloguing in Publication Data.
A catalogue record for this book is available from the British Library.

ISBN 0 7524 1847 5

Typesetting and origination by Tempus Publishing Limited.
Printed in Great Britain.

# Contents

Three signallers of the 1/4th Dorsets training in India, 1915.

# Introduction

The story of the Dorsetshire Regiment began in 1702 with the raising of a regiment by Colonel Richard Coote which became the 39th Foot (later 1st Battalion). It continued until their amalgamation with their West Country neighbours, the Devonshire Regiment, in 1958. The 39th won the honour PRIMUS IN INDUS for being the first British regiment to serve in India and distinguished itself at the battle of Plassey. Along with the 54th Foot, raised in 1755 and destined to become the 2nd Battalion, the two regiments served all over the world. In 1801 the 54th captured Fort Marabout near Alexandria and gained the title MARABOUT as a unique honour, still worn in the badge of the Devon and Dorset Regiment today. The 39th saw service in the Crimea while the 54th were in India at the end of the Mutiny. In 1881 the 39th and 54th joined together to form the Dorsetshire Regiment with its newly built Depot and barracks at Dorchester.

In the next seventy-seven years the Regular, Territorial and war-raised Battalions of the Dorsets were to see action in a variety of campaigns. Pte Samuel Vickery won the Victoria Cross in the Tirah campaign in India and both regulars and volunteers served together in South Africa. All of the major theatres of the First World War saw the Dorsets in action. France and Flanders, Mesopotamia, Gallipoli and Palestine all provided the Regiment with new Battle Honours. The inter-war years saw the Regiment dealing with rebellions in Malabar and Palestine while in the Second World War, the Regiment took part in three assault landings at Sicily, Italy and Normandy, the campaign in North-West Europe and the reconquest of Burma.

The photographs used in this book take up the story from 1859 with the early days of the Dorset Rifle Volunteers and continue through to the refurbishment of the Regimental Museum in the 1990s. There is not a wealth of photographs in the collection that date before 1881, as one would expect, but from the late Victorian period onwards the Regiment has been photographed in many places and in many activities. In the archives there are the accumulations of large numbers of posed groups and candid shots from barracks and camps all over the world but in amongst these are also a number of campaign photographs. Some of these have been included where perhaps their lack of quality or clarity is compensated for by the uniqueness of their time and place.

Not surprisingly a whole book could have been compiled using only the material relating to the Rifle Volunteers and the Territorials, not only at home but also in their valuable services overseas in two world wars. As such, a generous selection has been included as by the mere definition of these units, the individuals involved had very strong links to the county.

I have tried to include photographs that cover all battalions of the Regiment as well as most campaigns and peacetime activities but it has not always been possible to do this in a very balanced way. For example the museum holds hardly any original photographs of the Gallipoli campaign or of the 6th Battalion in France in the First World War. Even so there are some photographic treasures that have been captured by amateur photographers within the Regiment who could never have imagined the value or the interest that would be placed on their own or their contemporaries' snapshots in years to come.

Nearly all of the photographs presented here are from the regimental archives of the Keep Military Museum in Dorchester, the rest being taken from my own personal collection. Hopefully they will help to record moments in time in the regiment's history, illustrate specific uniforms and insignia, and say something about the military aspects of the county of Dorset.

I hope that the book will prove of interest not only to those having links with the Dorsetshire Regiment and to military students and historians, but will also appeal to those with a more general interest in, and an appreciation of, the magic of the captured photographic image.

Terry Bishop
Dorchester 1999

# Acknowledgements

I would like to thank the Trustees of the Keep Military Museum for permission to publish the photographs preserved in the museum. I am also grateful for the guidance and expertise provided by both Maj. T. Saunders MBE, Devonshire & Dorset Regiment, and Peter Smith, valued colleague and military researcher. I must also acknowledge the continual support that I receive from Lt-Col. N. Parmley and the staff and volunteers at the Keep. Finally a special mention must be made of the late Maj. L. Brown MBE, who provided much of the initial enthusiasm and encouragement for this project.

# One

# From Early Days
# to 1914

Officers of the 54th at Fort William, Calcutta, 1865. The following year the Regiment embarked for England after serving nine years in India. It was not a healthy tour and during that time, 5 officers and 376 men died – victims of dysentry, cholera, fever and sunstroke.

Capt. Henry Augustus Templer of the Dorset Rifle Volunteers. In 1859 as the Mayor of Bridport, Henry Templer raised the 1st Bridport Corps of the Dorset Rifle Volunteers, which he commanded for thirteen years.

The first camp of the Dorset Rifle Volunteers at West Lulworth in 1864. Capt. Henry Templer stands in the foreground with his charger. His groom stands close by.

No. 3 Corps of the Dorset Rifle Volunteers assembled in West Walks Dorchester for a day on the ranges. No. 3 Corps wore their own individual cap badge, which bore the arms of the Borough of Dorchester. In 1881 this corps was renamed 'C' Company, a title that Dorchester volunteers would retain up until 1915 when they were serving in India.

Sgt Barnard of the 54th Foot at the Curragh Camp, *c.* 1867.

Sgt M. Power of the 39th Foot at Fermoy, 1868.

Col.-Sgt Sprowle, 54th Foot, in Ireland, c. 1869.

The Corps of Drums 54th Foot, in Ireland in 1870. They wear kilmarnock forage caps with regimental numerals. These were replaced later in that year by glengarries. The Corps of Drums has its usual compliment of drummer boys, many of whom would have been born into the Regiment.

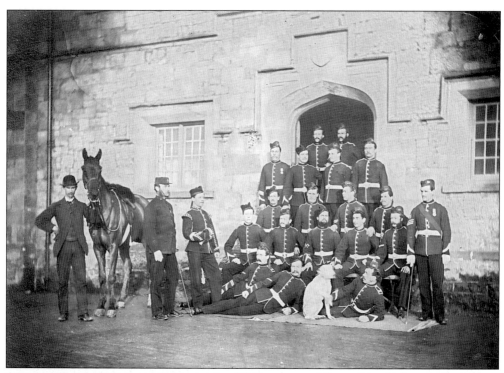

'E' Company soldiers of the 54th, outside their barracks at Ballina, Ireland, in 1870. The officer is Maj. J.W. Hughes, who as a lieutenant had been on the troopship *Sarah Sands* when fire broke out and the crew abandoned ship. Along with others of the 54th, he was especially commended for his actions in saving the ship. He eventually retired with the rank of Major General in 1884.

Paymaster-Sgt A. Allnatt of the 39th Regiment in India, *c.* 1875.

The Marabout Gun with men of the Depot Company, 54th Regiment, at Chatham in 1874. The gun was presented to the Regiment for its action in capturing Fort Marabout on 21 August 1801. The gun moved to the Depot at Dorchester where it was eventually put on display at the Regimental Museum.

Warrant Officers and Sergeants of the 2nd Battalion at Peshawar in 1885. Seated in the centre wearing caps are Sgt Major Barrett on the left and QMS Newsham on the right. Drum Major Paddy Maloney is standing at the rear with his mace. The star at the front was made by Colonel Gossett and consisted of old cap and collar badges of the 54th Foot.

Officers of the 39th Regimental Depot and the 3rd Battalion Dorset Regiment at Dorchester Barracks in 1885. The officer in the front, standing between the wheels of the gun carriage is Col. Henry Marshall, commanding 39th Regimental District. As can be seen from the different headgear and badges, several of the officers employed at the Depot were attached from other regiments.

Officers of the 1st Battalion in Cairo, 1891. In July 1889, the Battalion had been mobilized at Malta to proceed to Egypt to put down the renewed Dervish activity. By the time the Dorsets arrived, however, the troubles had subsided. The officers are wearing the 1881 forage cap badge that attempted to link the castle of the 39th with the sphinx of the 54th. It was never popular as a badge, however, and was replaced in 1893.

Pte Henry Phillips, 1st Dorsets, at Plymouth in 1892. Pte Phillips, a carter from Castle Cary, originally enlisted in the Dorset Militia in 1889. The following year he transferred to the 1st Battalion, serving in Egypt and India. He died of sickness while at Bangalore in April 1896, aged twenty-four.

Best shooting company of the 2nd Dorsets, 1895. Men of 'G' Company proudly display the Best Shooting Company Shield at Willow Bank in Belfast. The larger shield on the ground is for the Inter-Company Tug-of-War competition.

The 2nd Battalion on parade at Victoria Barracks, Belfast, in 1895. The mounted officer at the front is Lt-Col. Egerton who commanded the Battalion from 1891 to 1897.

Men of 'G 'Company, 2nd Dorsets, outside the armourer's shop and barrack store at Victoria Barracks, Belfast, in 1895. The men are involved in a variety of duties and pastimes ranging from Indian club swinging to playing draughts, alongside the ongoing cookhouse duties of fetching and preparing food, chopping wood and cleaning.

QMS Harry Lee, 1st Volunteer Battalion, who joined the Weymouth Company of the Dorset Rifle Volunteers in 1860. On 8 April 1895 he was presented with the Volunteer Force Long Service Medal. This photograph, taken two days after the presentation, shows him wearing his medal and standing next to his shooting trophies.

Trooping the Colour in Malta in 1897. During their two-year tour at Malta, the 2nd Battalion provided so many drafts for the 1st Battalion in India that the 2nd Dorsets were not included in the drafts of reinforcements sent to the Sudan in 1898. Despite consisting very largely of young soldiers, the Battalion did, however, send a detachment to Crete to quell the riot there of the Bashi-Bazouks.

Officers and Sergeants of the 1st Dorsets on campaign in Tirah, 1897. Left to right, back row: Sgt Coleman, Sgt Gardner, Col.-Sgt Pell, Sgt Collis, Sgt Russell, Sgt Tooley. Middle row: Sgt Searle, Signaller/Sgt Elderfield, Sgt Bidgood, Sgt Slade, Col.-Sgt Kemp, Sgt Hennesay. Front row, seated: Sgt Burbidge, Col.-Sgt Verdon, Lt Cowie, Lt Col Piercy, Col.-Sgt Giovanni, Sgt Moffat. On ground: Sgt Parmiter, Col.-Sgt Hawkins, Sgt Sheppard, Sgt Batten.

Lt H.N.R. Cowie, 1st Dorsets, dressed in an afghan coat and cap comforter in the Tirah, 1897. Lt Cowie was a distinguished officer in the campaign, being one of the first to reach the summit at Dargai. In South Africa he was awarded a DSO while attached to the 1st Devons at Ladysmith. He commanded the 1st Dorsets at Hill 60 in the First World War and was killed in action there on 5 May 1915. His death was described as 'the regiment's worst loss of the war'.

21

The armourer's shop of the 1st Dorsets in the field on campaign in 1897. The soldier in khaki drill working on the muzzle of the rifle is Armourer-Sgt Coleman.

An example of the animal transport hired by the 1st Battalion on the frontier to carry its stores. The poor condition of the beast is evident. The handler wears the curtain on his foreign service helmet to give additional protection to eyes and the back of the neck.

Samuel Vickery who won the Victoria Cross for outstanding bravery in the Tirah campaign. During the attack on the Dargai heights on 20 October 1897, Pte Vickery rescued a wounded comrade under fire. He subsequently further distinguished himself at Waran Valley where he was wounded. He received his medal personally from Queen Victoria at Netley Hospital after being invalided home.

The reception for L/Cpl Vickery VC at South-Western station, Dorchester, on 17 June 1898. Sam Vickery was to return to active service, with the 2nd Battalion in South Africa, where he was severely wounded causing him to be discharged in 1901. He returned to the Colours for the First World War, serving with the 6th Battalion in France, finally coming home in 1919.

A bridge construction party of the 1st Battalion, c. 1898. The insignia on the foreign service helmet is a left facing sphinx collar badge on a diamond shaped backing. This badge backing would have been green. Collar badges were worn for a short period as cap badges in the field service cap but metal badges were not often worn on the tropical helmet by the Regiment in this period.

A donkey polo match at Cherat. Below the carved badges on the Frontier, Sergeants of the 1st Battalion line up for a match against the officers in 1898. The picture captures the carnival atmosphere that filled these events. Seated on the ground in white are the regimental servants who wore a regimental badge in their turbans.

A posed group of 3rd Battalion soldiers at Hythe, c. 1899. On their epaulettes, other ranks wear the numeral 3 over 'Dorset'. The officer second from the left has the old badge of the Dorset Militia, a stork which was the crest of Lord Rivers, on his FS cap.

The cyclist section of the 1st Volunteer Battalion at Aldershot in 1899. It was felt that the use of cycles would enhance the effectiveness of Volunteer Force units and compensate for the lack of cavalry. Cyclists' main roles were to take messages and carry out reconnaissance.

Bandsmen of the 2nd Battalion at Shorncliffe in May 1899. They are, left to right: L/Cpl Paskett, Dmr Newman, Sgt-Dmr Drew, Boy Rennie, Cpl Sparrow. Sgt-Dmr Drew wears the 'Station Masters' pattern forage cap while the musicians wear the coloured field service cap. The uniforms have white facings which all line regiments had to adopt in 1881. They were not replaced by regimental coloured ones until 1904.

Officers of the 2nd Dorsets at Shorncliffe prior to their departure for South Africa. Colonel Law, the commanding officer is seated fifth from the left. After mobilization, the Battalion left Southampton aboard SS *Simla* on 24 November 1899.

On campaign at Wakkerstrum, South Africa, in March 1900. Col. C.H. Law, is seen sitting third from the right, along with the officers of the 2nd Dorsets.

The Volunteer Service Company about to leave for active service at Dorchester in 1900. Volunteer units were formed to reinforce their regular battalions but were able to serve as a discrete company. The majority of the company came from the Volunteer Battalion, but their numbers were made up with men of the Dorset RGA Volunteers. Lt Lano of the Royal Garrison Artillery is seated in the centre wearing the dark uniform. To his left is Capt. Kitson who commanded the company.

621

Wimborne volunteers bound for South Africa. These are members of 'F' Company, 1st Volunteer Battalion, who volunteered for active service in 1900. They are, left to right: Pte G. Bulgin, Pte G. Burden, L/Cpl C. Stride, Pte F. Walker, Dmr J. Frizzell, Pte C. Randall, Pte S. Beament, Pte A. Ellis, Pte F. Phippen.

The Dorchester contingent of the Volunteer Service Company at the barracks, prior to leaving for South Africa. Seated in the centre is Sgt Medway. In front of him is Bugler 'Dolly' Stevens whose father was the Bandmaster of the Volunteer Battalion.

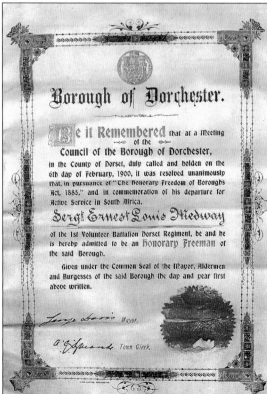

### Borough of Dorchester.

**Be it Remembered** that at a Meeting of the Council of the Borough of Dorchester, in the County of Dorset, duly called and holden on the 6th day of February, 1900, it was resolved unanimously that, in pursuance of "The Honorary Freedom of Boroughs Act, 1885," and in commemoration of his departure for Active Service in South Africa.

**Sergt Ernest Louis Medway**

of the 1st Volunteer Battalion Dorset Regiment, be and he is hereby admitted to be an **Honorary Freeman** of the said Borough.

Given under the Common Seal of the Mayor, Aldermen and Burgesses of the said Borough the day and year first above written.

*George Davis* Mayor.

*A. Symonds* Town Clerk.

A scroll conferring the honour of Freeman of the Borough of Dorchester on to Sgt E. Medway, for volunteering for active service. Seventeen men from Dorchester, serving in the Volunteer Battalion saw service in South Africa and each one was made an Honorary Freeman of the Borough.

'F' Company of the 2nd Dorsets on Grass Kop, South Africa, 22 July 1900. The Dorsets are photographed under heavy shell fire from the Boers in the plain below, but the shelling on this day was quite inaccurate as shown by the relaxed attitudes of the soldiers.

The 2nd Battalion leaving Zand Spruit for Ingogo, Natal, on 3 August 1900.

Men of 'F' Company, 2nd Dorsets, helping the Navy to move their guns on 14 September 1900. They are seen manhandling a naval 12 pounder into position at Partridge Hill, South Africa.

Sgt T. Panter on campaign in South Africa. Acting as a mounted infantryman, Sgt Panter illustrates the newly adopted uniform style of the British Army on active service against the Boers.

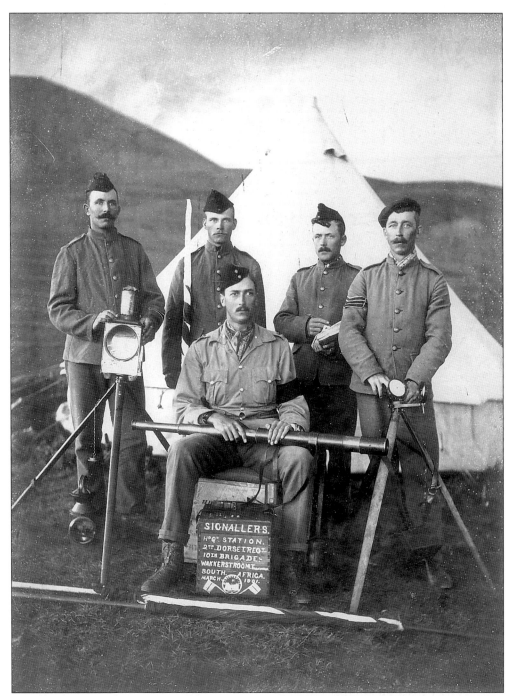

Signallers from the 2nd Dorsets in South Africa in 1901. The signalling officer, Lt Frank Hill, was commissioned in 1895 and saw action in the Tirah. In the Boer war he played a vital part in maintaining lines of communication and was awarded the DSO for his services. He later transferred to the Royal Fusiliers.

A decorative arch erected in South Street, Dorchester, to welcome home the 2nd Battalion from South Africa. After disembarking at Southampton, on 19 October 1902, the Dorsets were given an enthusiastic welcome from the people of Dorchester and an elaborate reception by the local dignitaries.

Unveiling of the Tirah Commemorative Obelisk in Dorchester Borough Gardens, 24 May 1900. The memorial was unveiled by the Earl of Ilchester and lists the names of the twenty-three soldiers who lost their lives in the Tirah Campaign.

Colours of the 1st Battalion being laid up in Sherborne on 19 May 1901. On either side of the Guard of Honour are men of the 1st Volunteer Battalion in darker rifle green uniforms. In the distance can be seen the Abbey and the large building in the middle distance is the Digby Hotel.

The 1st Battalion on the great parade ground at Nowshera, India, 1900. On this occasion officers and men of the Battalion were presented with the 1895 India Medal for their services in the Tirah.

The presentation of South African war medals to the men of the 2nd Dorsets at the Depot, Dorchester, in 1902.

Dining outside for soldiers of the 1st Battalion in India, *c.* 1904. When the Battalion finally returned home, in 1906, it had served for nearly nineteen years abroad; having left England in 1888.

Working in the garden in India, *c.* 1905. With the combination of isolated postings and a strong temperance movement within the British Army, spare time activities like gardening proved popular. Two of these 1st Battalion soldiers are wearing the unpopular Broderick cap, which was in service until 1906.

Officers of the 1st Battalion at a break during a training exercise in Bombay, 1904.

Depot Sgt-Maj. Benjamin Verdon DCM, 1904. Enlisting in 1883, Col.-Sgt Verdon served in the Tirah and then went to South Africa with the Volunteer Service Company as their Colour Sergeant where he won the Distiguished Conduct Medal at Alleman's Nek. On his return he served as Sergeant Major at the Depot until he was discharged in 1908.

Decorations in the 1st Dorsets camp in preparation for the great review at Rawalpindi, December 1905. This was in honour of the visit of HRH the Prince of Wales, later to become King George V.

The nominal roll of the 1st Battalion, a combined embroidery and drawing produced by Sgt-Drummer Clark in 1905. It contains the names of all the officers and men serving with the Battalion in Ferozepore at that time.

Club swinging class of 'B' Company, 2nd Dorsets, at Colchester in 1905. The soldiers are wearing the circular cap badge that was worn from 1895 to 1906 and embroidered 'Dorset' shoulder titles with the Battalion number underneath. Some of the 'old sweats' unofficially held onto these cap badges as a sign of long service well into the First World War.

The Company shots of the 1st Battalion in 1906. Left to right, standing: Pte Simmons, Cpl Broomfield, Pte Cummings, Cpl Parker, Pte May. Seated: Sgt Heathman, L/Sgt Sharpe, L/Cpl Pitman, They are wearing the 1903 pattern leather bandolier equipment.

Regimental signallers of the 1st Battalion at Ferozepore, Punjab, in 1906. In command is Lt E.J. Hewitt who had been wounded during the Tirah campaign. In 1914, at the outbreak of war, he was transferred to the newly raised 5th (Service) Battalion. He later became a Brigade Staff Captain but returned to the 1st Battalion to command it for a few months in 1916. He retired in 1923 as a Lieutenant Colonel.

Instructors of the 1st Battalion at Ferozepore. They are, left to right: Sgt-Dmr Clarke, Schoolmaster Mr Crisp, Gymnastic Instructor Sgt Fitch, Sgt-Maj. Hunter, Signalling Instructor L/Sgt Tuck, Capt & Adjt A.L. Moulton-Barrett, Drill Instructor Sgt Wood, Bandmaster R.J. Shepherd, Musketry Instructor Sgt Heathman.

The regimental workshops of the 1st Battalion in India. This posed group illustrates the variety of activities carried out by the craftsmen in the Battalion. Trades ranging from armourers to printers and carpenters to signwriters all supported the Battalion on a daily basis.

Unit transport for the Volunteers: a steam lorry carrying men of the 1st Volunteer Battalion on camp at Minehead, 1906. They are wearing a mixture of new khaki serge and the old rifle green uniforms. The two soldiers sitting at the rear of the lorry wearing service dress caps are Army Service Corps Volunteers attached to the Battalion.

Col. C.H. Law's final parade on 24 November 1906. The occasion was to distribute Long Service & Good Conduct Medals at the Depot. Commissioned as an ensign in 1869, Col. Law went on to command the 2nd Battalion in South Africa and in 1903 he took command of the 39th Regimental District.

A rear view of the Keep at Dorchester in 1908. A sentry box stands next to the Marabout gun as the keep was the guardroom for the Depot. The low walled structure to the right is the exercise yard for prisoners detained in the guard room cell.

'The Boys of the Old Brigade': veterans of the Crimea, Indian Mutiny and Abyssinian campaign assembled at Blandford, on 11 September 1907, the 50th anniversary of the siege of Delhi.

Competitors from the 4th Battalion in the King's Final at Bisley, 1908. Seated at the front is Sgt Green from Gillingham, while at the back centre is L/Cpl Samways from Dorchester and standing on the right is Sgt Dickinson from Sherborne.

The Colour Party of the 4th Dorsets (TF) in 1909. The party was among 108 Territorial Force units that received colours or guidons from HM King Edward VII at Windsor on 19 July 1909. The Colour Party comprises, left to right: RSM Joy, Col.-Sgt Knight, Lt Fletcher, Col.-Sgt Bridle, Lt Whetham, Col.-Sgt Bower.

The Maxim gun section of the 4th Dorsets (TF) at annual camp, Windmill Hill, 1909.

NCOs of the 2nd Battalion in possession of the Long Service and Good Conduct Medal at Poona in 1911. Most had served in the Boer war and at the time their combined service totalled over 197 years. They are, left to right, back row: Col.-Sgt Leach, Col.-Sgt DeLara, Col.-Sgt George, Col.-Sgt Abbot, Col.-Sgt Williams. Front row: Col.-Sgt Watts, BandMaster Hazell, Sgt Major Alderman, Col.-Sgt Seamark, Col.-Sgt Hayden.

Pte William Nobbs, 1st Dorsets, as a mounted infantryman in Aldershot, c. 1911. On his right arm he wears the fleur-de-lys, signifying that he was a first class scout. The five-pointed star meant that he was proficient in judging distances. Pte Nobbs, from Branksome, went to France with the 1st Battalion and died of wounds in February 1915.

The Depot at Dorchester in 1911. Built in 1879, the Keep was the gateway, guardroom and arsenal for the new barracks, which formed a square behind it. Like all regimental depots, its main function was to train new recruits prior to their postings to the regular battalions.

The Dorset National Reserve at Fordington, Dorchester, in 1912. The NR comprised ex-members of all volunteer and regular forces who shared a patriotic urge to take part in operations on the outbreak of any war.

A group of the Dorset National Reserve in Weymouth, 1912. In January 1913, there were 3,101 ex-officers and men registered with the Dorset NR. National Reservists did not wear uniforms – only a button hole badge. In Dorset this badge was an enamel circle surrounding a head of a Dorset Horn ram.

Volunteer Service Company men still serving in 1912. Stalwart members of the 4th Battalion (TF), they all proudly wear their Queen's South Africa Medals. The Private standing on the extreme left wears the Imperial Service brooch above his right tunic pocket. This signifies that he has volunteered to serve overseas in time of a national emergency.

Sgt Scott's shooting team, 'C' (Dorchester) Company, 4th Dorsets (TF), 1912. Left to right, standing: Pte R. Foster, Pte Hurst, Pte C. Eady, Pte J. Joy, Pte T. Dowd, Pte S. Howe, Pte H. Barnes, Pte E. Wilson. Sitting: Pte B. Norris, Sgt C. Old, Sgt A. Scott, Cpl H. Moore, Pte M. Gilday. Sgt Scott wears his Volunteer Long Service Medal, which was awarded to him in 1909. A fishmonger by trade, he enlisted in 1896.

The first dinner of the Dorset Old Comrades Association on 6 December 1913. It took place in the town hall, Dorchester, and was attended by ninety-two old comrades including ex-Cpl Vickery VC.

L/Cpl W. Jones of 1st Dorsets, c. 1913. L/Cpl Jones went to France with the Battalion on 16 August 1914 and was subsequently commissioned in November 1917.

L/Cpl G. Constable, 1st Dorsets, seated by his postcard collection in his barrack room, c. 1913. He went to France in August 1914 with the BEF but died back in the UK in April 1915.

Recruits undergoing physical training at the Depot under the supervision of Sgt-Instructor Stephens in May 1914. The photograph was taken from the roof of the Keep and clearly shows the Little Keep at the other end of the parade ground. This group of buildings had been built in 1866 as the Dorset Militia HQ.

The Officers' Mess of 'A' (Bridport) Company, 4th Dorsets. Pictured on a weekend training near Burton Bradstock in 1914, the officers are, left to right: Capt. H.E. Duke, Capt. L. Whetham, Capt. H.L. Kitson, 2nd-Lt A.C. Tucker, Lt J. Roper, Lt K. Suttill. Capt. Kitson commanded the Volunteer Service Company in South Africa, while Capt. Whetham had served there as a Sergeant.

A friendly boxing match between members of the 4th Battalion (TF) at Sling Plantation, Bulford, at the start of their annual camp in late July 1914. Within a week they had mobilized for war.

The machine gun section of the 4th Dorsets (TF) in training at Bulford Camp, July 1914. The Sergeant nearest the gun is from the 4th Wilts (TF). The Wilts Territorials, the 4th Dorsets and the 4th and 5th Somerset Light Infantry formed the South-Western Infantry Brigade of the Wessex Division and trained annually together.

# Two

# The Great War

Reservists being detailed to Companies within the 1st Battalion at Victoria Barracks, Belfast, 7 August 1914. Between the outbreak of war and 9 August, the 1st Battalion received 572 reservists from Dorchester. The efficient mobilization put the Battalion up to war strength so that on 14 August it embarked on the SS *Anthony* for France.

Volunteers for the 5th Dorsets at Dorchester in early August 1914. In response to Kitchener's call for volunteers for a New Army, recruits flooded into Dorchester, the vast majority being Dorset men. On 28 August the newly raised Service Battalion went to Belton Park, Grantham, to begin training as part of the 11th (Northern) Division.

Left to right: Capt. Ransome, Lt Pitt and Sgt Boater march in a party of reservists at Victoria Barracks, Belfast, on 7 August 1914. The reservists reported for duty at Dorchester, then were sent in drafts to Belfast to join the 1st Battalion.

Col. F.G. Wheatley recruiting soldiers for the New Army in Poole, September 1914. He had previously served in the Dorset Rifle Volunteers from 1881, taking command of the Battalion in 1907 as it evolved into the Territorial Force. He retired as a Lt-Col. in 1912.

Wimborne Company of the 4th Dorsets (TF), about to leave for India on mobilzsation in 1914. Territorials were only liable for home service but the War Office decided that if two-thirds of officers and men in a battalion would volunteer to go overseas, then the Battalion could serve as a complete unit. The 4th Dorsets volunteered and were accepted for service as the first line or 1/4th Territorial Battalion of the Dorset Regiment.

Men of the Weymouth and Portland Companies of the Dorset National Reserve forming up at Weymouth station shortly after the outbreak of war. This was the sixth draft of volunteers for Kitchener's New Army to be provided by the Dorset NR.

Headquarters servants of the 1st Battalion at a halt during the retreat from Mons at Crepy-en-Valois, 31 August 1914. The Battalion retreat, which took place between 21 August and 5 September, covered 220 miles in the 16 days. The forced march took place in very hot weather and 50 per cent of the Battalion were reservists.

Lt R.E. Partridge, at 5.30a.m. on 2 September 1914, after a night's rest under a haystack. This picture was taken on the 1st Dorsets' retreat from Mons, about 25 miles East of Paris. The stack was Battalion HQ bivouac for the night.

The troopship SS *Assaye* which carried part of the Wessex Division including the 1/4th Battalion to India. Leaving Southampton on 9 October 1914, she landed at Bombay on 10 November. Out of respect of the 39th's honour PRIMUS IN INDUS, it was arranged that the 1/4th Dorsets were the first Territorial battalion to disembark onto Indian soil.

Taking on coal for the SS *Assaye* at Port Said, 22 October 1914. To many of the Territorials on board, the voyage to India was quite an adventure as many had never even been outside their own county before.

The arrival of the 1/4th Battalion (TF) at Ahmednagar, 15 November 1914. The Dorsets were met at the station by three military bands who marched them the four miles to camp, where they were welcomed by Gen. W.H. Dobbie. The Dorsets then took over garrison duties at the large internment camp there.

'C' and 'D' Companies of 2nd Dorsets being towed by HT *Varela* prior to landing in Mesopotamia, 6 November 1914. They landed at Fao, prepared for opposition, but the Turkish defenders had rapidly moved out as the boats neared the shore.

Cooks of the 2nd Battalion in their makeshift shelter at Basra in December 1914. Occupying the Custom House in Basra, the Battalion only remained there for six weeks before advancing north.

Two men of 'D' Company, 1st Dorsets, writing letters home in January 1915. They are in the fire trench near the Wulverghem-Wytschaete Road. At this time the system of work in the 15th Brigade was that each battalion spent three days in the front line and three in reserve.

The 1st Dorsets holding 15A Trench opposite Wytschaete in February 1915. The German trenches were just by the trees in the centre of the picture.

Officers of 'D' Company, 1st Dorsets, January 1915. This photograph was taken at Burnt Farm, near Wulvergham church about 500 yards from the front line. Pictured are, left to right: Lt Wheeler, Lt Wood (standing), Capt. R.E. Partridge (commanding 'D' Company), Lt Morley.

The 1st Battalion manning 38 Trench at Hill 60 in the spring of 1915. The soldier seated in the middle is holding a makeshift periscope with which he can view the enemy trenches. It was opposite these trenches, on 1 May 1915, that the Germans launched a devastating gas attack.

Officers of 5th (Service) Battalion at Belton Park, March 1915. Left to right, back row: 2nd-Lt Le Cornu, 2nd-Lt Montgomery, 2nd-Lt Dymock, Lt Higgins, 2nd-Lt Drysdale. Middle row: 2nd-Lt F. Smith, 2nd-Lt L. Smith, 2nd-Lt Richards, Lt Hill, 2nd-Lt G.W. Smith, Lt Bowler, 2nd-Lt Schulze, 2nd-Lt Grant, Lt Cook, Lt Clayton. Front row: Lt Horton, Capt. Gregory, Capt. Hewitt, Maj. Day, Lt-Col. Hannay, Maj. Leslie, Capt. Le Marchant, Capt. & Adjt Carruthers-Little, Capt. Vincent. At the front, on ground: 2nd-Lt Bare, 2nd-Lt Ford, 2nd-Lt Jones. Of this group of officers, five were later to die in the war, eleven were wounded and four were invalided home.

Men of 'C' Company, 5th Battalion, in training on a route march near Grantham early in 1915. The troops display a variety of equipment typical of the Service battalions who started training without even having uniforms. In April 1915 the Battalion moved to Witley Camp to complete its training prior to going overseas.

Sergeants of the 6th Service Battalion at Bovington, early in 1915. the majority of them were 'old sweats'. After training, the Battalion landed in France on 14 July 1915 as part of the 17th (Northern) Division, serving there for the rest of the war.

Pte Ernest Burt, 2/4th Dorsets 1915. A typical joining up photograph, this was taken when he was in billets in Winton. Pte Burt, from Winterborne Monkton, went as a draft to the 2/4th Battalion in India and then on active service with them to Palestine. On the disbandment of the Battalion, he was transferred to the Machine Gun Corps.

A concert party of the 1/4th Dorsets at Ambala, October 1915. This was a very popular diversion for the Battalion and they gave fortnightly concerts. The pierrot sitting in the centre is CSM George Wright from Dorchester and standing centre is CQMS Charles Cook from Poole.

Bandsmen of the 2/4th Dorsets enjoying a brew at teatime in the band's tent in India, 1915.

A draft of the 1/4th Dorsets under Capt. C.W. Symes leaves Dagshai as reinforcements for the 2nd Dorsets in Mesopotamia. The men reached the 2nd Battalion in May 1915 in time to take part in the action at Ctesiphon and the withdrawl to Kut.

'C' Company, 2nd Dorsets, digging defensive positions at Shaiba, Mesopotamia, in March 1915. The Dorsets prepared for an anticipated attack down the River Euphrates which came on 13 April 1915. The Dorsets played an important part in the action and a charge by them against the Turks eventually secured success, but at the cost of many Dorsets including the CO Col. Rosher.

The RMS *Aquitania*. On 2 July 1915, the 5th (Service) Battalion, comprising 29 officers and 875 other ranks s embarked at Liverpool for Lemnos, landing nine days later. For many Dorset soldiers on board the *Aquitania*, the experience of travelling on the great Cunard liner was very memorable though it was soon to be overshadowed by the action at Gallipoli.

The charge of the 2nd Dorsets on the redoubts outside Kut al Amara. On 28 September 1915 the Dorsets faced stubborn resistance from a well armed and well entrenched enemy. The part they played in the success in taking Kut on that day won them eight Distinguished Conduct Medals.

The Arch at Ctesiphon where, on 22 November 1915, the 6th Indian Division won a costly victory over the Turks in the allied advance on Baghdad. The 2nd Dorsets suffered a fifty per cent casualty rate and Gen. Townsend realized that as Turkish reinforcements were getting closer, the position could not be held. The Division then started to withdraw to Kut al Amara.

A group of 1st Battalion soldiers in France probably late in 1915. As part of 14th Brigade in the 32nd Division, they wear on their arms the battalion insignia of a red diamond above two horizontal bars. The bars were in various colours indicating the particular company.

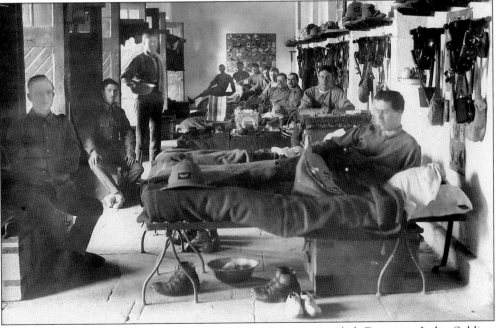

The sleeping accommodation for men of 'D' (Poole) Company 1/4th Dorsets in India. Soldiers are opening their parcels from home as this was taken at Amballa at Christmas 1915.

The Sergeants' Mess of 1/4th Dorsets at Amballa on Christmas Day 1915. Seated centre in the front row is RSM Harold George. A regular soldier, at the outbreak of war he was Col.-Sgt Instructor with the Gillingham Company of the 4th Batallion. On mobilization of the first line Territorial Battalion, he was appointed RSM.

A typical example of the souvenir postcards available to British troops in France. This has an inserted photograph of an unidentified soldier of the 1st Dorsets. At this stage in the war, it seemed highly unlikely that the the fighting would continue until 1918.

For gootness sake go back! Here kom der DORSETS

A postcard of the early First World War period, mixing humour with patriotism. This one was posted from Bovington Camp, in 1916, where the 7th (Reserve) Battalion of the Dorsets were stationed.

A street in Kut al Amara during the siege in the spring of 1916. The siege lasted from 7 December 1915 until 29 April 1916. Despite repeated rescue attempts, Gen. Townsend was forced to surrender due to lack of food and medical supplies.

The 2nd Dorsets at a church parade during the siege of Kut al Amara. The Dorsets lost 3 officers and 39 men in the siege. When the town fell to the Turks, 12 officers and 400 other ranks were taken into captivity. By the end of the war only the officers and 120 men had survived.

A programme of events for the 'Kut Fund Day'. The fund raising day, on 26 July 1916, centred around a procession of motor cars decorated to represent allied nations and patriotic characters. Australian Imperial Forces stationed at Weymouth provided a band and a company of recovered wounded ANZACs paraded through Dorchester.

Kut Day in Dorchester, 26 July 1916. Following reports of the captivity of so many Dorset men on the fall of Kut, a fund raising day was arranged in Dorchester. Weymouth and Bridport followed suit and in 1916 the three towns had raised over £1,600 for comforts for the prisoners of war.

The Band of the 3rd Battalion at Wyke Regis in 1916. The 3rd Battalion lost its Militia title in 1907 and became 'Special Reserve'. As such the 3rd Dorsets lost any chance of seeing service overseas as an operational unit, but instead did excellent work throughout the First World War in carrying out training and finding drafts for active service units.

No. 1 Platoon, 2/4th Dorsets, take an elephant ride on a visit to Mankote in August 1916. Throughout 1916 the Battalion was stationed at Jullundar in the Punjab, moving to Bombay the following year from where it sailed for service in Palestine.

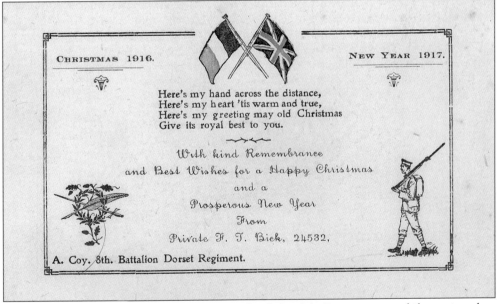

A personalized Christmas card from Pte Bick of the 8th Dorsets, sent while stationed at Blackpool. The Battalion had started its life as the 2nd (Home Service) Battalion, becoming the 8th in November 1916. It existed for another year, primarily for training and to find drafts for other battalions.

Officers of the Dorsetshire Volunteer Regiment, *c.* 1916. Standing second from the left is Lt O.C. Vidler, machine gun officer, and in the centre is Capt. G. White. The Volunteer Regiments were set up for men unable to meet either physical or age requirements of the armed forces. They provided their own uniforms and rank was shown by the braid on the cuffs. Volunteer Regiments took over much of the home defence role of the Army, especially in the latter stages of the war.

The machine gun section of the Dorset Volunteer Regiment at Templecombe on 29 April 1917. On this day the Regiment was inspected by Field Marshall French. Two officers and 915 NCOs and men were on parade accompanied by the Weymouth Volunteer Brass Band.

Men of the 1/4th Battalion entraining at Nasiriyeh, ready to leave for Basra on 29 March 1917. The railway, which had only been opened at the end of 1916, greatly speeded up the movement of troops through Mesopotamia.

A sketch of the monument to the fallen at Ramadi, Mesopotamia. Ramadi garrison was taken by the allies on 28/9 September 1917 and the 1/4th Dorsets were prominent in the action. Copies of this sketch were made available to men of the 15th Division who had fought there. This copy was brought back by Cpl Fred Atkins of Stinsford, who saw action there with the 1/4th Battalion.

The arrival of Pte Inwood at the 1/4th Dorsets camp at Ramadi, 11 October 1917. Pte Inwood of the Hants RFA had been captured on the fall of Kut. He had eventually escaped into the desert by stealing a horse and had joined up with a group of Armenians before coming across the Dorset camp.

Lt H.L. Watkins having a shave after a halt on the march of the 2nd Dorsets in Mesopotamia, late in 1917.

Men of the 2nd Dorsets taking cover during a Turkish air raid in slit trenches at Samarrah, Mesopotamia, in the winter of 1917.

Men of the 1/4th Battalion preparing for a twenty-four-mile march on 27 March 1918, the day after the battle of Khan Baghdadi. The aim was to take on the remaining Turks, but shortly after the photograph was taken, news was received that the Turks in the area had surrendered. This was greeted with loud cheers.

Dishevelled men of the 1/4th Battalion resting at a halt on the march on the road between Khan Baghdadi and Ramadi on 12 April 1918. The men had been campaigning for two months without a change of clothes and so, on reaching Ramadi, the men had disinfectant baths and their clothing had to be boiled.

Dorset and Hampshire soldiers of the North Russian Relief Force on formation at Crowborough in April 1919. The unit was formed to help relieve British troops stationed in Russia and to support the White Russians. The Dorset men came from the 1st Battalion in Londonderry and formed 'Y' Company of the 2nd Hampshires. For uniformity all companies wore the Hampshire cap badge once the unit was operational.

# *Three*
# Between the Wars

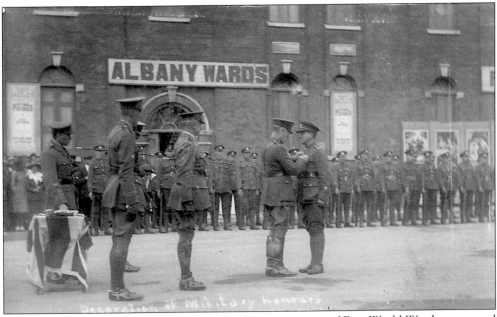

The 2nd Battalion on parade in Portland for the presentation of First World War honours and awards on 28 July 1919. Gen. Jackson is making the presentation with the CO, Lt-Col. Radcliffe, standing behind him.

Regimental Provost Staff of the 2nd Battalion in Bangalore, 1919. In the centre is RSM Bolingbroke who had originally been in the Norfolk Regiment, but acted as RSM of the composite 'Norsets' in Mesopotamia. He subsequently became RSM of the 2nd Dorsets and was commissioned in 1921.

RSM Wells and the 1st Battalion Regimental Police in Ireland, 1920. On the outbreak of war, Wells was serving on the permanent staff of the Depot but was soon transferred as an experienced NCO in to the 5th (Service) Battalion, where he served with distinction in Gallipoli and France, winning the MC and the DCM. He became RSM of the 5th Battalion and at the end of the war returned to the 1st Dorsets.

The band, drums, flutes and bugles of the 2nd Battalion at Bangalore, 1921. Bandsmen wear dark green cords and two green folds are worn in the pagri of 2nd Battalion Wolseley helmets.

Moplah prisoners being guarded by men of the 2nd Battalion in Malabar, 1921. The Dorsets were mobilized in August 1921 to help quell the uprising of the fanatical Moplahs, as they were the nearest British infantry unit available. By the time the Battalion left Malabar in November, the rebellion was quietening down, but it had proved quite a difficult operation for the Dorset soldiers.

The 2nd Dorsets in action against the Moplahs at Melmiri Mosque on 25 October 1921. 'A' and 'D' Companies carried out the attack supported by one section of 10th Pack Battery RGA and four armoured cars of the Royal Tank Corps.

Detraining at Bangalore after the operations in Malabar, 21 November 1921. The officer of the 2nd Dorsets not wearing webbing is Lt D. Stephens.

'A' and 'D' Companies, 2nd Dorsets, marching into Baird Barracks, Bangalore, on returning from Malabar, 21 November 1921.

Officers of the 2nd Dorsets at Bangalore, November 1921. This group photograph was taken on the return of the Battalion from Malabar. They are, left to right: Capt. D.A. Simmons, Lt-Col. C. Saunders (CO), Capt. J. Bessell (Adjt), Bvt Lt-Col. G.M. Herbert, Lt J.S. Hewick.

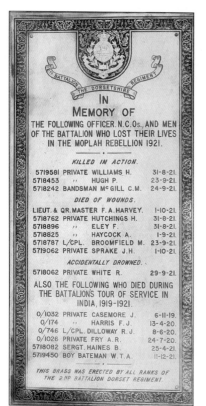

IN
MEMORY OF
THE FOLLOWING OFFICER. N.C.Os., AND MEN
OF THE BATTALION WHO LOST THEIR LIVES
IN THE MOPLAH REBELLION 1921.

*KILLED IN ACTION.*

| 5719581 | PRIVATE | WILLIAMS H. | 31-8-21. |
| 5718453 | ,, | HUGH P. | 23-9-21. |
| 5718242 | BANDSMAN | McGILL C.M. | 24-9-21. |

*DIED OF WOUNDS.*

| LIEUT. & QR. MASTER F. A. HARVEY. | | | 1-10-21. |
| 5718762 | PRIVATE | HUTCHINGS H. | 31-8-21. |
| 5718896 | ,, | ELEY F. | 31-8-21. |
| 5718825 | ,, | HAYCOCK A. | 1-9-21. |
| 5718787 | L/CPL. | BROOMFIELD M. | 23-9-21. |
| 5719062 | PRIVATE | SPRAKE J.H. | 1-10-21. |

*ACCIDENTALLY DROWNED.*

| 5718062 | PRIVATE | WHITE R. | 29-9-21. |

ALSO THE FOLLOWING WHO DIED DURING
THE BATTALION'S TOUR OF SERVICE IN
INDIA, 1919-1921.

| O/1032 | PRIVATE | CASEMORE J. | 6-11-19. |
| O/174 | ,, | HARRIS F.J. | 13-4-20. |
| O/746 | L/CPL. | DILLOWAY R.J. | 8-6-20. |
| O/1026 | PRIVATE | FRY A.R. | 24-7-20. |
| 5718082 | SERGT. | HAINES B. | 25-4-21. |
| 5719450 | BOY | BATEMAN W.T.A. | 11-12-21. |

*THIS BRASS WAS ERECTED BY ALL RANKS OF
THE 2ND BATTALION DORSET REGIMENT.*

A memorial plaque to members of the 2nd Battalion who lost their lives in the Moplah rebellion. A tragic loss to the Regiment was that of Lt & QM Harvey. As RQMS he had been captured at the fall of Kut, in 1916, and did great service to his fellow captives. The plaque was erected in the Garrison church, Bangalore.

Dorset Old Contemptibles still serving in 1923. These all went to France with the 1st Battalion in 1914 and wear the 1914 Star. They are, left to right, back row: Chick Davis, Harry Bowen, Jack Chick, Henry Newton. Middle row: Sgt Banbury, Sgt Pope, Sgt-Dmr Prowse, Sgt Smith, Sgt Thompson MSM. Front row: CSM Creech DCM, Lt & QM Stehr MSM, Col Ransome DSO MC, RSM Ball MSM, CSM Cannings DCM.

Vickers machine guns and associated equipment in the MG store of the 2nd Battalion in Khartoum, 1922. The Dorsets remained at Khartoum for sixteen months during which time they were put under orders to move to Constantinople. The orders were cancelled, however, and so the Battalion missed out on an unusual posting for a British regiment.

The Royal Guard to HM the King at Aldershot for the presentation of new Colours to the 2nd Battalion, 11 June 1924. The officer in command is Lt K.W. Wright. The presentation was to have taken place on Laffan's Plain but bad weather forced the ceremony to be moved to the Central Gymnasium in Aldershot.

Col. Radcliffe presenting Indian General Service Malabar medals to the 2nd Battalion at Aldershot, 6 June 1925. RSM Hatton is seen receiving his medal.

The band of the 2nd Battalion on a summer tour of Southern England. The band is pictured at Herne Bay, where they played in June 1929.

The departure of the 2nd Battalion from Germany for home on 28 September 1929. The symbolic lowering of the union flag at Bad Schwalbach was carried out by Lt Bolingbroke and coincided with the end of the Army of Occupation in Germany by British forces.

The four Regimental Sergeant Majors of the Regiment serving in 1930. Left to right: F.J. Edwards (1st Battalion), F. Gilchrist (2nd Battalion), H.J. Hatton (Depot), J. Scott (4th Territorial Battalion).

Soldiers from 1 and 2 Platoons 'A' Company, 4th Dorsets (TA), prepare to board their charabanc in Bridport to go on camp in the summer of 1930.

Winners of the Regimental Davidson Cup medals for rifle shooting, May 1931. Pictured at Chakrata, India, they are, left to right, standing: Bdsm Edwards, RSM Edwards, Cpl Smith, Pte Clatworthy. Seated: Pte White, 2nd-Lt A.D. Ward, L/Cpl Pugsley (winner of cup), Boy Trist.

The bed space of Pte Reynolds of the 1st Battalion with kit laid out ready for inspection, *c.* 1935. Everything had to be polished or pressed and on display in the prescribed fashion. Hanging in front of Pte Reynold's squared sheets and blankets is his regimental bed plate stamped with his name and number.

A group of 1st Battalion men in India, *c.* 1936. They are wearing the new, lighter, tropical helmet that replaced the Wolseley helmet. Cap badges were worn on the helmets for parades and formal regimental duties.

The Regimental Band leading the 1st Battalion into Landi Kotal at the Afghan end of the Khyber Pass. Arriving in 1936, the Battalion stayed there for a year where it took advantage of the topography to become proficient in mountain warfare.

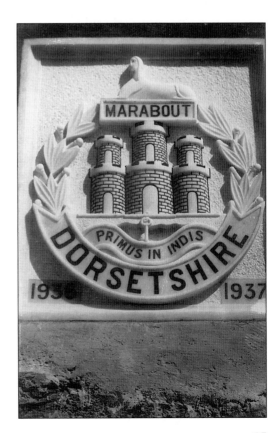

The regimental badge in the Kyber Pass, near Landi Kotal. Erected in 1937, it was made of Agra marble and cost 310 Rupees or £23.

The CO and men of the 2nd Battalion in Palestine, 1936. They are, left to right, standing: Cpl Ross, Pte Windsor, Pte Garghan, Cpl Horlick, Pte Dawson, Pte King, Capt. E.J. Bullard. Seated: Maj. E.L. Stephenson, Lt-Col. C.H. Woodhouse. The Battalion's time in Palestine was arduous but luckily there were few casualties.

A Lewis gun section of the 2nd Dorsets guarding the Palestine broadcasting station at Ramallah during the Arab Rebellion in 1936.

Tirah veterans at the memorial obelisk in Dorchester to commemorate the fortieth anniversary of the storming of Dargai, 20 October 1937. Left to right, back row: Pte E. Rollins, Pte E. Syms, Pte J. Hoddinott, Pte F. Tizard, Pte A. Gawler. Front row: RQMS J. Swain, Pte J. Bowring, Pte H. Farnham, Lt-Col. L.C. Hope, Brig.-Gen. C.C. Hannay, Sgt J. Thurley.

Soldiers of the 1st Battalion forming up after detraining in India, *c.* 1937. Despite being issued with the new lighter tropical helmet, they are still carrying their old Wolseley helmets in covers on their large packs.

A certificate presented to Pte A. Taylor of the 2nd Battalion on leaving the regiment after seven years service. These colourful certificates were popular with many regiments in the 1930s.

No. 8 Platoon, 'B' Company, 1st Dorsets, in training in the hills above Landi Kotal in 1937.

Soldiers of the 1st Battalion patrolling the North-West Frontier, c. 1938. The machine gunner is armed with a Vickers-Berthier Light machine gun. Although never universally accepted by the British Army, the Indian Army had adopted this weapon in 1933 as the replacement for the Lewis gun. It was soon to be superseded however by the Bren gun.

MT Section of the 4th Dorsets (TA) at annual camp, Windmill Hill, in August 1938. The vehicles appear to mainly be 15cwt Morris Commercials.

*Four*

# The Second World War

No. 21 Platoon, 'C' Company, at the Infantry Training Centre, Poundbury Barracks, Dorchester in 1940.

A platoon of 4th Dorsets (TA) in training at Berkhamstead, summer 1940. The Bren gunners carry around their necks the Bren wallet containing tools and spare parts. The 4th Battalion eventually landed in France as part of 43rd Wessex Division on 23 June 1944.

The parade of the 70th (Young Soldiers) Battalion, Dorset Regiment, at Gosport in 1941. Formed in 1940 from young soldiers of the 6th (Home Defence) Battalion, it was reorganized as a field force unit in 1943 and re-designated the 9th Battalion. It eventually became the demonstration battalion for the School of Infantry.

The departure of 'F' Company, 6th Dorsets, from HMS *Raven*, Eastleigh, in 1941. The Company had been formed from volunteers of the 81st Defence Group to guard vulnerable points in the south of England. Re-designated 30th Battalion in 1941, it was mobilized in 1943 and went overseas to continue its guard duties in Sicily and Gibraltar.

Lads of the MT section 4th Dorsets (TA) at Herne Bay, 1941. After mobilization, in 1939, the Battalion went into a period of training mainly in the south east of England that was to last until June 1944.

Men of 1st (Bridport) Company, Dorset Home Guard, *c.* 1943. Dorset units wore the letters 'DOR' above their Battalion number on each arm of their battledress blouse. D-Day meant the removal of invasion threats and so the Home Guard was officially stood down on 1 November 1944, with final disbandment coming in 1945.

Men of the 2nd Battalion, Dorset Home Guard, relaxing after a parade, *c.* 1943. Dorset raised seven battalions of the Home Guard of which the 2nd was the Dorchester Battalion.

No. 3 Platoon, 'A' Company, 4th (Sherborne) Battalion, Dorset Home Guard, c. 1943. The curious weapon at the front is the Spigot Mortar, which could fire a 14lb bomb nearly 800yds.

Bringing Dorset to India at Gulunchi Camp, July 1943. This was a training camp used by the 2nd Dorsets prior to them advancing into Burma in 1944. A feature of camp life was for battalions to provide local name signs to the camp roads. Two of the soldiers wear the popular bush hat that the whole battalion was wearing by mid-1943. The crossed keys of 2nd Division was worn on the left, while the battalion flash of LIV (52nd) was worn on the right.

The vital road junction at Kohima which was fought for by 'A' Company of the 2nd Dorsets on 27 April 1944. Under vicious enemy fire, the company held on for a week before being relieved. The action at Kohima was a turning point in the campaign as it stopped the movement of Japanese forces into India along the Manipur Road.

D-Day on 6 June 1944. The 1st Dorsets are leaving *Empire Crossbow*, the mother ship, about ten miles off the French coast at 5.45 a.m.

Heading for the beach. An evocative photograph, one of a series taken by Capt. G.G.L. Hebden, shows the inside of one of the 1st Dorsets landing craft on the way in on 6 June.

Pte B. Childs, 1st Dorsets, who was wounded on D-day. This photograph of Pte Childs, who was Capt. Hebden's batman, was taken just before he went back to the Regimental Aid Post for treatment.

Capt. Hebden in front of a knocked out Panther tank, Normandy, on 15 June 1944. The previous day, Capt. Hebden and some of the 1st Battalion anti-tank platoon had immobilized this tank with their 6 pounder anti-tank gun.

A day at the races for men of the 2nd Battalion: home-made entertainments to celebrate 'Sarah Sands' day at Maram Camp on the Manipur Road, November 1944. This was a period for the Dorsets to re-organize and refit prior to crossing the Chindwin for the advance to recapture Burma.

The edge of the Reichswald in February 1945. A 6 pounder anti-tank gun team of the 4th Dorsets in February 1945. The action here, against determined opposition, was to last for a month, but by the end of it, the allies were firmly in control of the Rhine approaches.

Three members of the 4th Dorsets anti-tank platoon stand in front of their Bren gun carrier in Germany in the spring of 1945. They wear the Cap General Service, an unpopular forerunner to the general issue of the beret in the British army. As a regimental distinction, the Dorsets wore a green backing to their cap badge in the GS cap.

Sergeants of the 9th Dorsets at Sheringham in June 1945. The Battalion formed part of 220th Brigade that provided five weeks Reserve Division training to soldiers prior to going overseas. The trainees on courses came from both the Dorsets and the Norfolks.

Men of 5th Dorsets anti-tank platoon awaiting the attack on Ahausen, 23 April 1945. Left to right: Cpl Hervey, Pte Hughes, Pte Warton. By nightfall the Battalion was established in the village and eighty prisoners had been taken.

The end of the war in Europe: soldiers of the 5th Dorsets relaxing at Kuhstedt, 5 May 1945. Left to right, standing: Pte Holmes, Pte Tipper, Pte Curtis, Pte Folly. On the carrier: Pte Carpenter, Pte Worton, Cpl Hart. At the time of the German surrender, the Battalion was the nearest British troops to the enemy and so on that fateful day they found themselves the focus of attention of the press.

The 5th Battalion officers outside their mess at Hotel Tostedter Hof, Tostedt, Germany shortly after VE Day in June 1945. Left to right, back row: Lt Weller, Lt Farmer, Lt Smith, Lt Rowe, Lt Coley, Lt Hudson, Lt Andrew, Lt Tonge, Lt Montford, Lt Dyne. Middle row: Capt. Levy, Capt. Grimsdell, Capt. Pratt, Capt. Hitches, Capt. Riley, Capt. Aspinall, Capt. Thomas, Capt. Fisher. Front row: Capt. Meads, Capt. Dawes, Capt. Edwards, Maj. Roe, Lt-Col. Bredin DSO MC, Maj. Pack, Capt. Hodges MC, Capt. Docherty, Capt. Betts.

# Five

# Peacetime and Amalgamation

Signal platoon of the 2nd Dorsets at Matsue, Spring 1946. As part of the occupation force of Japan, the soldiers wear the Union Jack flash of BRINDIV on the right arm and the crossed keys of 2nd Infantry Division on the left.

The last march past of the 5th Dorsets on their final parade at Spandau, Berlin. The disbandment date for the battalion was 30 June 1946, after which it was put in to suspended animation like many of the duplicated wartime territorial battalions.

Sentry duty for the 2nd Dorsets at the Imperial Palace, Tokyo, in July 1946. As part of the British Commonwealth Occupation Force, the 2nd Battalion became the first regular British battalion to visit the Japanese capital. Of the eleven posts for guard duty around the palace, five of these were shared with the US Army.

Passing out parade at the 39th Dorset County Primary Training Centre. Marching past, on 25 February 1947, is Maj. A. Thomas, Maj. J. O'Driscoll, Sgt Leith and Cpl Gill. Brig. C.H. Woodhouse is taking the salute. PTCs were set up in 1946 to give initial training for to those called up for National Service. During their stay, recruits were medically examined, given six weeks basic training and selected for arm of service before being posted to their respective training units.

No. 14 Platoon, 'C' Company, 2nd Dorsets, at Batu Pahat, Malaya, in the spring of 1947. 'C' Company was on detachment to Batu Pahat to primarily guard the vehicle park there which housed over 4,000 military vehicles.

The 1st Dorsets on Operation Woodpecker in Germany in 1947. In the last three months of 1947, the whole Battalion was involved in this operation which entailed felling thousands of tons of timber from the forests of Northern Germany and loading it onto rail. This timber was then shipped to the UK to help in the rebuilding of Britain.

Dorset soldiers sawing timber on Operation Woodpecker in 1947. Working with other British Army units, the Battalion took part in this work of national importance, producing timber for house building and pit props. During the three months of the operation, which took place during a very severe winter, 253,000 tons of timber was felled.

Colours of the 2nd Battalion being taken into the Officer's Mess at the Depot, 6 January 1948. Post-war defence cuts called for the reduction in infantry battalions and so the old 54th were reduced to a cadre. The colours were paraded for the last time in 1948 through Dorchester and then were finally laid up.

The Sergeants' Mess of the 1st Battalion, (39th and 54th) Dorset Regiment, on the amalgamation of the 1st and 2nd Battalions in Vienna, 1949. The picture shows the wide variety of styles of battledress being worn at that time. Officers and Warrant Officers wear their blouses open at the neck with collar and tie. As a regimental distinction, not only was a green badge backing worn on the GS cap and the beret, but it was also worn behind metal badges of rank.

A royal visit to the Depot on 3 July 1952. Her Majesty the Queen, accompanied by Maj. P.J. Roper TD, inspects the guard of honour of the 4th Dorsets (TA). The visit to the Depot and the Regimental Museum formed an important part of the 250th anniversary celebrations.

The surviving members of the Volunteer Service Company at the Dorchester Cenotaph, July 1952. Left to right: Joe Matthews, Jim Forse, George Smart, A.B. Holder, Jim Frizzell, Algy Price, Lt Wheatley, Ted Jukes, Capt. Kitson, Bill Read, Brig Woodhouse (Colonel of the regiment), C. Stride, Charles Ingram, Herb Pover, Jack Rowan, Bill Porter, Jim Traves, Ted Gatehouse.

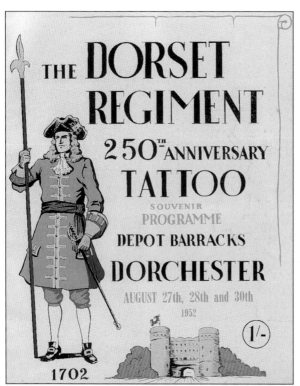

A souvenir programme of the 250th anniversary of the raising of the 39th Regiment by Colonel Richard Coote. The events in August 1952 included searchlight tattoos and a regimental cricket week culminating in a drumhead service at the Regimental Depot.

The visit of the 4th Dorsets (TA) to 60th AA Battery, US Army, Lakenheath. The visit took place during annual camp at Stanford in May 1953. The Dorset Territorials at that time wore the 43rd Wessex Division Wyvern on the right arm and the cross of the Wessex Brigade on the left.

Kohima Camp guardroom, Korea, 1955. The guard provided by 'D' Company, wears summer dress. The NCO in the doorway is Regimental Provost Sgt D. Field. The guardroom itself was entirely built by battalion labour.

The anti-tank platoon in Korea. Armed with Battalion Anti-Tank guns (BATs) and Browning machine guns, the platoon is commanded by 2nd-Lt P.S. Groom.

The 3in mortar platoon, Dorset Regiment in Korea in 1955. The platoon is commanded by Lt A.R. Tawny. The Korean soldiers in the group are KATCOMs, other ranks permanently attached to the Battalion. Wearing Dorset insignia, they were fully integrated being divided up among all companies and departments.

Preparing to move into the Demarkation Zone in Korea in the spring of 1955. To operate in the DMZ, patrols had to wear MP headress and armbands plus white cross straps. The men from 'C' Company are, left to right: Pte Rickards, KATKOM Wo-Hi-Moon, Pte Vanstone, 2nd-Lt Bembridge, Pte Rowe, Cpl Smith.

The successful 4th Dorsets (TA) China Cup team at Bisley, 1956. Left to right, standing: L/Cpl B. Ainsworth, Sgt K. Nicklen, Sgt B. Bearne, Cpl R. Goodwin, Pte A. Wareham. Seated: CSM E. Chivers, Lt-Col P.J. Roper TD, RQMS J. Felton, CSM J. Stubbington. The trophy is for an annual competition for Volunteers and Territorials, dating from 1864. The 4th Dorsets winning score in 1956 was the second highest on record at that time.

HRH The Duchess of Kent inspects the guard of the 4th Dorsets (TA) at Dorchester. Her visit on 7th July 1956 was for the presentation of new colours to the battalion.

The end of the Depot Barracks at Dorchester. The depot closed in 1958 as amalgamation meant that RHQ moved to Exeter. In 1960 the barracks were sold off to Dorset County Council and the Royal Mail, with the Keep being retained as the regimental museum. Buildings not required were demolished.

The three Colonels at the amalgamation of the Devons and the Dorsets. Left to right: Maj.-Gen. G.N. Wood CB CBE DSO MC, (Colonel the Devonshire and Dorset Regiment), Lt-Col G.R. Young OBE, (Commanding 1st Battalion Devonshire and Dorset Regiment), Col. L.H.M. Westropp DL, (Late Colonel the Devons).

Amalgamation Parade, Minden, on 21 May 1958. On formation of the Devonshire and Dorset Regiment, the cap badge of the Wessex Brigade was adopted along with new Devon and Dorset shoulder titles. Shortly after amalgamation the regiment was to take part in its first operation during the emergency in Cyprus.

The Keep at Dorchester in the late 1990s. It is now the Military Museum of Devon and Dorset, displaying artefacts from seven of the regiments that were raised within the two counties and maintaining and preserving the regimental archives. After a major refurbishment, the title 'The Keep Military Museum' was adopted in 1994.